Hello My Name Is Committed:

Stories About Dealing with Mental Illness in Student Affairs

A COMPILATION OF STORIES FROM
STUDENT AFFAIRS PROFESSIONALS
ABOUT MENTAL ILLNESS

HELLO
my name is

Committed

EDITED BY KRISTEN ABELL

ILLUSTRATED BY SUE CAULFIELD

TOM KRIEGELSTEIN & SABINA DEMATTEO
· BOOK EDITORS ·

Hello My Name Is Committed:

Stories About Dealing with Mental Illness in Student Affairs

Collaboratively Created By

Kristen Abell – Series Editor

Sue Caulfield – Illustrator

Tom Krieglstein – Book Editor

Sabina De Matteo - Book Editor

Other Student Affairs Collective Books

Beyond Meetings: Lessons and Successes in Advising Student Organizations

Men in Student Affairs

From the Beginning: Perspectives from New and Emerging SA Pros

All titles can be viewed and ordered at

www.StudentAffairsCollective.org/Bookstore

A Student Affairs Collective Book - Volume 2

Hello My Name Is Committed: Stories About Dealing with Mental Illness in Student Affairs

Printed in the United States of America

Design by Student Affairs Collective

10 9 8 7 6 5 4 3

Student Affairs Collective

www.StudentAffairsCollective.org
info@studentaffairscollective.org

Phone: (877) 479-4385

Fax: (206) 337-0259

>> Contact for bulk order discounts <<

About The Student Affairs Collective

As with all great ideas, the Student Affairs Collective (www.StudentAffairsCollective.org) began as a series of doodles on the back of a napkin by Tom Krieglstein & Kevin Prentiss in 2005. The vision was, and still is, to create the ultimate online community of Student Affairs Professionals in which everyone is both a teacher and student at the same time to help each other play, learn and grow together to collectively reach higher levels of success.

In the beginning, Tom and Kevin wrote all the content. They then bribed their Student Affairs friends with cookies and digital unicorns to help them write more content, and slowly, over time, an engaged community developed. The SA Collective started to become the go-to place online for Student Affairs professionals to receive and share knowledge from their peers. The growth remained steady, and then Twitter came along...

In 2009, over lunch with Debra Sanborn at an Iowa coffee shop, Tom pitched the idea of a weekly chat via Twitter for Student Affairs professionals. Debra nodded excitedly at the idea (as she does with all new ideas), and a couple weeks later, on Oct 8th, 2009, the first #SAChat happened with 15 people and 50 tweets.

Since then, the SAC, which is what the cool kids call it, has grown to be a community of thousands of Student Affairs professionals, stretching international borders and all functional areas of the field. We now have a podcast, a book club, a jobs board, a member directory with learning communities, a weekly newsletter, Tweetups, and the #SAChat Awards. Through it all, the

SAC continues to focus on creating the best online, low cost, peer-to-peer learning network for Student Affairs professionals.

Now it's your turn to jump in and be a part of the family and help us create the next ten years of awesomeness. As a bonus, you'll laugh, smile, create friendships, and grow a positive national reputation for yourself and your work. Then, when you go on to change the world, we'll get to say you first shared your potential with us by helping fellow Student Affairs Professionals be even more amazing!

How To Use This Book

While this entire book in focused around one main theme, each individual author takes on a unique perspective around the main theme. Some chapters might be totally relevant to your current situation and others not so much. Reading this book from beginning to end is probably not going to be as valuable as looking at the Table of Contents and skipping ahead to the chapters that are most relevant to your current situation.

Share The Love Online

We love seeing when fellow Student Affairs Professionals take their professional development into their own hands. If you take a photo of you with this book and share it online via one of the channels listed below, we'll send you a special little gift in return!

On Twitter post your photo using one of these two methods:

> Use the #SAChat hashtag
> Tag the @The_SA_Blog account

On Facebook post your photo to one of these two groups:

> Student Affairs Professionals >
> https://www.facebook.com/groups/2204795643/
> Student Affairs Collective >
> https://www.facebook.com/SACollective

To the contributors.

Simply put, this book would be nothing without you.. Thank you for saying yes to the first email (and every one after!). Thank you for sharing your story and then continuing the conversation, both on and offline. We hope that you know how much of a difference you have made and how grateful we are for your bravery.

To the collaborators.

This book is a dream come true. Thank you to Tom, Sabina and the Student Affairs Collective for dreaming with us and being a supportive venue to host our eSeries. Without you, Committed would not have had the home that it did.

Thank you to everyone who has participated in the #SAcommits conversation online, and particularly for anyone who has taken it offline. The continuous knowledge, sharing and supportive nature of this little feed lifts us up in so many ways.

To the next chapter,
Kristen & Sue

Kristen's Acknowledgements

To my partner in life and crime, Sean, for putting up with me, for taking care of me, and for standing up for me when I can't stand up for myself - I am a lesser person without you. and to my little light, Aedan - you amaze me daily, and I hope someday you will understand all of this better and not have to fight the same fight.

To all my friends and colleagues who have struggled - or are still struggling - with mental illness. in many ways, this series was inspired by you. I hope for health for you and that you will one day be able to live without stigma.

To my friends and colleagues that have read my (too) many blog posts on this subject. you inspire me to keep writing and sharing the message.

And finally, to Sue. if you keep reading, she's going to tell you she couldn't have done this without me, but the truth is, she's pretty freaking amazing all on her own. This series started as her idea, and it definitely wouldn't be what it is without her ability to illustrate all of our thoughts. In the past year, we have become collaborators, co-conspirators, and most amazing of all - good friends. I'm a better person for having you in my life, friend. Here's to more crazy ideas ahead of us.

Sue's Acknowledgements

To all my student affairs friends, suedles exist because of your encouragement. Thank you for all of your support. To Amma, thank you for opening my eyes and being my partner. To Chris, this one is for you.

To my dad Jim, thank you for teaching me to 'be the light' and to push myself to do things I never thought I could do. To my mom, Angel, thank you for encouraging my creativity and for always listening. To my sister Kerri, and my brother Tim, thank you for always making me laugh & keeping me on my toes. Celebratory dinner?

To Dan, thank you for dealing with me, for loving me and for pushing me to be a better person. I know I can do anything with you in my corner.

Finally, this journey would have never started without Kristen. Thank you for helping me sort through my thoughts when I told you I had this vague 'idea for a comic about mental health.' Thank you for steering me in the right direction, for sharing the excitement, laughs and tears. Most of all, thank you for your incredible editing skills. This entire series would have not made sense without you (literally). We did it, cofounder & friend.

table of contents

introduction.

Caretakers. On call staff. Front line folks. The people who wear multiple hats.

From generalists to specialists to somewhere in between, student affairs professionals serve in every unique role that you could think of on a college campus. We provide services and resources to students in need. We seek out at risk students and have a knack for checking in at just the right time. We provide tools for development and encouragement for the future.

We spend our days honed in on the needs of our students and fail to see the needs of ourselves.

The truth is, our colleagues are not always fine. Our job titles are not "student affairs robots" or "student affairs superheroes." The more we pretend those are our titles, the less progress we will make in battling the stigma around mental illness in student affairs.

In the past few years, discussions around mental illness in student affairs have been in and out of the spotlight. In November of 2013, Huffington Post published an article entitled "Student Affairs Administrators Get Suicidal, Too." Kristen Abell, co-founder and editor of this series has written about her struggles with depression on her personal blog. However, it was a tweet from Stacy Oliver that helped us decide to make this discussion a little more prominent.

"Remember those 4 days we were all riled up and adamant we were going to talk more about mental health in #studentaffairs? #sachat" - @StacyOliver

In honor of National Mental Health Awareness Month, and with the help of the Student Affairs Collective, Kristen and I launched the e-series "Committed." Our goal was to put mental health in the spotlight and keep it there. We hoped that by sharing the stories of other student affairs professionals, consistent conversation could be created surrounding mental health.

This book is a compilation of twenty stories from student affairs professionals from various places, backgrounds and experiences. Their eagerness to share their stories proves at least one thing - that consistent conversation around mental health and student affairs professionals is desperately needed. We hope this book can serve as a resource and a source of hope for our field.

Cheers to being Committed,

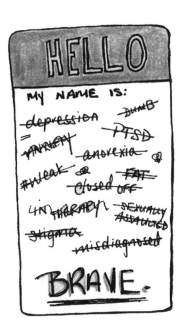

May is Mental Health Awareness Month, and we want to take this time to recognize those among us who have been affected by mental illness. Sue Caulfield, student affairs professional and creator of the popular Suedles, along with Kristen Abell, student affairs professional and blogger, have coordinated a series of blog posts with illustrations to highlight this important issue for the month of May. We all hope to make mental health for student affairs professionals an ongoing focus of our profession and not just a one-shot topic.

STOMPING out Stigma - Kristen Abell

I started writing about my struggles with depression on my personal blog in 2007, but it was several more years before I outed myself to the student affairs community. I can still remember the churning in my stomach and the cold sweat I broke into after hitting "publish" on my post. I can remember the overwhelmingly positive response I got from those who commented, shared, or emailed me privately to thank me for the post. **I also remember the silence from people I had hoped and thought would respond - in a way, that spoke louder than the comments from those that supported me.**

Someone recently asked me if I regretted posting so publicly about my depression. I know why they asked that, but it makes me sad that there was a reason for them to ask. I know there are many people - even people reading this - that think I should be ashamed of my depression, that it makes me weak, that it makes me less than them. I used to believe that myself.

But here's the thing - my depression does not define me. **I am more than my illness.** And I am angry.

I am angry that we let mental illness define who a person is - and we view them and treat them as an other - as different from us. **I am angry that there are people who believe that one person should be able to talk about their physical ailments but think I should shut up about my mental illness.** I am angry that we can talk 365 days a year about being fit and physically healthy, but we only get one month for mental health.

It is not enough for us to say that we support those with mental illness - we must show it. We must make this an ongoing discussion - not just on Twitter, not just on blogs, but in our offices, in our families, in our lives. **We must acknowledge the stigma that surrounds mental illness, and then we must stomp on it.**

Over the next month, several brave individuals will be sharing their stories on this blog. I hope that you will read them with kindness and compassion. I hope you will not fear asking these individuals how they are doing in the future. I hope you will not be afraid of them or feel sorry for them.

And then, then I hope that you will use this month as an impetus to educate yourself and those around you on the realities of mental illness. I believe it is time for us to acknowledge this as more than a one-time topic, time for us to acknowledge this as a part of all of our lives.

Are you ready to take steps to learn about and educate others on mental health? Here are a few ideas to get you started.

1. Organize a "lunch & learn" and share this blog post to start the conversation on your campus.
2. Work with your health services or counseling office to host a mental health screening or other educational event.
3. The hashtag for Mental Health Month is **#mhmonth2014** - or use **#sacommits** if you want to talk about mental health in student affairs on Twitter; check out the Mental Health Month Facebook page; or join the American College Counseling Association on LinkedIn. If you're not on social media, send an email to three people and ask for their thoughts.

Join me this month - this lifetime - in stomping out the stigma of mental illness.

Kristen Abell is a web developer at the University of Missouri-Kansas City and has been in student affairs in a variety of positions for about 15 years. She has been fighting (and winning) a battle with depression for most of her life. Connect with her at @Kristen_Abell on Twitter or read her blog at kristen-abell.com.

misdiagnosed.

Stacy's Story

Misdiagnosed - Stacy Oliver-Sikorski

Blinking slowly, I regained consciousness on the floor of the bathroom in my Residence Director apartment. I remembered walking in there minutes before and leaning against the counter, hoping to ease the pain that was gripping my ribs like a belt cinching tighter and tighter as my breath became shallower.

It didn't make sense. These were the symptoms my doctor diagnosed as gallbladder attacks, culminating in my having my gallbladder removed. Was there such a thing as phantom gallbladder attacks? It seemed unlikely, but there also wasn't any other plausible explanation as far as I was concerned.

It would take more than three years before someone would put a name to these incidents. I didn't talk about them with friends, family, or doctors. But in the summer of 2008, I had a similar incident, and because I lost consciousness in a more public place, sought medical attention at the insistence of those who were with me at the time. After a series of tests, including an EKG, my physician sat down with me and started asking me questions about stress, anxiety, sleep habits and caffeine. As we talked about the things going on in my life and my general anxiety levels, she raised the notion that this could be a panic disorder. She provided me with multiple resources and encouraged me to connect with a therapist to better understand the disorder and how to manage it.

It took me another three months to call a therapist, to screw up the courage to admit I needed help managing my anxiety because it was impeding my relationships and my ability to do my job. When I connected with Rachel, who was my therapist for three years, she assured me that while a panic disorder and anxiety may not be normal, they are both manageable. **And they would both be more manageable if I let other people in and asked for help**.

I can't predict when a panic attack will occur; panic disorder is complicated by the anxiety caused by the unpredictability of the disorder. It creates a self-perpetuating cycle of sorts — I worry about panic attacks, which are relatively infrequent, but then I'm trapped in a cycle of anxiety.

So what helps? Meditation. Breathing exercises. Exercise.

And my partner, Dan.

Dan is phenomenal in the moments of a panic attack (among many other times). If we're apart from one another, he'll stay on the phone with me until the panic passes. If we're together, he'll hold my hand and talk quietly to me while I try to regulate my breathing. He knows when it's gone too far and I'm in danger of losing consciousness.

I always feel like Paul Harvey sharing the rest of the story when I tell this part, the serendipity that brought TallDan and me together —

Dan and I met via an online dating site. I initially ignored his outreach message, deeming him too tall for me. After my gallbladder surgery, when I was confined to the couch and growing increasingly bored, I responded to his message. Were it not for my misdiagnosed gallbladder, I may have never found the person who is my source of comfort and peace in moments that are sometimes terrifying and isolating. I'm fond of saying that I believe the universe gives us the people we need when we need them — and how could I believe anything different?

 Stacy Oliver-Sikorski is the Associate Director of Residence Life for Student Success at Lake Forest College, where she oversees housing operations and serves as the senior hearing officer. Outside of work, she enjoys baking, writing, and editing. Follow Stacy on Twitter @StacyLOliver. Or visit her personal website at www.stacyloliver.com

THE OTHER SIDE.

Sean's Story

The Other Side - Sean Grube

As many of you may know, my lovely partner, Kristen Abell, is a persistent advocate for mental health in the student affairs field. She's extensively documented her own battles with depression. I've been asked to talk about what it's like to be a partner (hopefully a supportive one) to someone that lives with depression.

First and foremost, it needs to be said that in our family, depression tends to be an ocean tide – it ebbs and flows. It might be tempting to assume that Kristen's depression impacts me daily, but I tend not to see it that way. For the most part, Kristen and I live our lives as an engaging couple with a stubborn eight year old and a spoiled dog. **There are good times, and there are difficult times, just as there are in any relationship.**

It feels a bit obnoxious for me write about how my partner's depression affects me. **It does impact me, but Kristen is the one that's battling through a really difficult situation, and I consider my own emotional state a distant second.** I guess that's a pretty apt description of how I approach those difficult days. In the nearly fifteen years that I've been with my lovely partner, there has probably only been a total of eight or nine months where I could really feel Kristen's depression. My partner is sad sometimes, it's difficult for her to do some things, and there is occasionally a bit of an emptiness in our house.

When Kristen is having a tough time navigating through her depression, it's natural for me to have some feelings of sadness or self-pity. I've come to believe that in those times, I'm starting to feel the weight of her depression (admittedly, just a small fraction of it). I think because the burden isn't mine to bear, I'm able to unload it a little easier than Kristen. I'm not sure that will make sense to everyone, but it's the best description I can provide.

However, more than anything, I reflect on memories of the strength and love in our family. My tendency is always to be the fixer, and I know that isn't what my partner needs or wants during those tough times. **So I direct my "fixing" to the things that I think will make our family feel better.** I make sure my partner knows that she is needed and loved. I make sure and talk to my son about how his momma is feeling. It's not easy for an eight-year-old to understand depression, but the one thing our family absolutely wants to avoid is pretending everything is okay or trying to hide Kristen's mental health.

I certainly don't have a magic bullet. Overall, I would say that I just try to be a good partner. Sometimes Kristen is sad, and sometimes it's tough for her to see the other side of the sadness. Sometimes it's tough for me, too. We talk about those things, we find a way to make it through the gloom, and we talk about making tomorrow a little bit brighter than today. It's seldom easy, but we've always managed to get to the other side.

Sean Grube is Director of Residential Life at the University of Missouri - Kansas City and has worked in higher education his entire career. He's a partner, father, and triathlete. Founding member of the Bald and Beautiful Society. Connect with him at @grubester on Twitter.

mindFULL - Lisa Endersby

I don't measure my weight on a scale much anymore. I measure my heaviness by my mood.

For as long as I can remember, anxiety has been an old friend, a constant companion and my worst nemesis. It's fascinating and frightening to watch other people be seemingly 'normal' as they go about their lives, so quick to recover from what you know isn't anywhere near the end of the world and so steady in their good moods. **Over time, I've realized that appearances can be deceiving, and we all certainly fight our own battles, but logic and objective judgment don't stand a chance in the face of the monster that is anxiety.**

For me, it's an overwhelming sense of dread coupled with knowing with absolute certainty that you are not enough - not smart enough, not good enough, not pretty enough - not enough to make it, do well and be worthy of love. What makes it worse is having conversations with your anxiety, knowing it intimately and understanding its triggers and motives. Sometimes, I find myself wishing I was truly 'insane' and living in the blissful ignorance of my mental mess, not knowing or caring about what was wrong with me. At times, it feels worse to know you're anxious and know you have mental health challenges because in your weaker moments, you long to be "normal," to be like "everyone else." It's a vicious cycle: getting anxious and then feeling bad about yourself for being anxious. Those closest to me sometimes don't know how to help, and, to be honest, many times I don't know either.

My mind and I often play a crude game of chess with each other, a game whose rules I still don't understand because they change at any moment, for no reason and without warning. I spend some days navigating the battlefield that is my mind, being careful to not step on any anxiety landmines that are artfully hidden and packed with emotional explosives. Over time, I've built a strong support system and found people and things that help me cope, but there is always the real danger of slipping back into old habits. I say habits because, as bad as the anxiety can be, it is still comfortable and safe. These days, I have the frustrating challenge of worrying when I'm not anxious. Something must be wrong if I'm happy or excited and simply in some state of calm and peace. **Without the anxiety, who am I?** Anxiety is safe enough for me to hide in, latching onto a twisted sense of pride when the other shoe drops because I knew it was coming. If you don't get your hopes up too high, you won't have far to fall.

I've found that being open about my struggles with people I trust has been helpful and therapeutic - it has led to some amazing conversations that I cherish to this day. I've given up wishing this will go away, and I am a lot better now than I was years ago at "taming the beast." I've focused my energy on looking for community and sharing my story; sharing not for pity or voyeurism but to let others know they're not alone. It isn't a competition to see who has it the worst but an opportunity to normalize what is a difficult and still stigmatized topic of conversation.

I know that I have good qualities, that I'm a good person and that I'm more than my anxiety. I only wish that I could know that all the time. **I continue to push forward, wanting to carpe every diem, even when some of those diems leave me breathless and afraid.** If nothing else, I hope others can know that they are not alone if they struggle too. One thought that comes to mind is the term "kintsukuroi" which comes from the Japanese and means "the art of repairing pottery with gold or silver and understanding that the piece is more beautiful for having been broken.

Thanks for letting me tell my story.

 Lisa Endersby has trouble standing still, sometimes because her mind runs faster than her legs can keep up. Working in student affairs for over 5 years, she has been honoured to inspire and share students' stories and is ready to share more of her own. You can connect with Lisa on Twitter at @lmendersby or hear more from her at www.lisaendersby.ca.

Surviving and Thriving as a Caregiver - Mallory Bower

In the beginning, things were just a little off. If you weren't close, you wouldn't have noticed. My intuition was in overdrive and my gut was screaming, "This isn't right!" But still, I couldn't quite put my finger on it.

First, there were the tall tales that I so badly wanted to believe. Elaborate stories, spun carefully with conviction and woven with lies.

Then there were bouts of hyper, all-in mania that made my head spin trying to follow along and make sense of it all. Hundreds of projects started but never finished. Nuts and bolts; screws loose.

Next came the mood swings, broken glass, unbridled anger. Followed by self-loathing and isolation.

And then, quiet. The calm before the storm that would brew again without warning.

The story about being diagnosed with bipolar disorder is not mine to tell. My story, the one about love, forgiveness, and being a caregiver, is one that I own but don't often share. Twelve years ago, I was too young to understand it and too young to be the glue that held us together. **Picking up the pieces took its toll on my own wellness, and in retrospect, I wish I had more information and support to thrive in my environment.**

One in four Americans suffers from mental illness. If you're not one of them, it's likely that someone in your household is. In our profession and in our lives we are often designated as caregivers, which can be both rewarding and stressful. Here are some quick tips on how to prioritize your own wellness when caring for others:

Arm yourself with information. Research your loved one's disease so you know how to identify symptoms and triggers.

Say "yes" to help from others. Keep a handy list of ways that friends and family can assist you. Trust me, no amount of help is too small or will go unnoticed.

Take time for yourself. I'm sure you've heard the phrase, "You can't care for others unless you care for yourself." This can be difficult for people in student affairs, even for individuals without caregiving responsibilities. Take a walk, meditate, exercise, or spend time with people who make you laugh.

Focus on what you can control. Don't spend too much time on the "what ifs?" Identify what is in your scope of control and do your best with everything else.

Know your limits and signs of burnout. Have a plan to refresh (see: "Take time for yourself"). Ask your friends and family members to step up so you can recharge your batteries and take care of your own mental wellness.

Seek counseling. Set up a regular time to chat with a therapist about your feelings and responsibilities. Find a support, and connect with people in similar situations.

Forgive your loved ones. Forgive yourself. It's so easy to harbor feelings of resentment towards the person for whom you're caring. I haven't quite mastered this one myself - but try your best to let go of and forgive behaviors that are beyond their control.

And most importantly, know that you are not alone.

 Mallory is a university career coach and friendraiser who's on a mission to find out what makes people "tick." Connect with her on Twitter (@MalloryBower) and via her blog (mallorybower.com).

EVERY TIME YOU SMILE.
Ryan's Story

Every Time You Smile - Ryan Bye

Smile. Just smile. You repeat this over and over in your head until you can't remember which muscles you need to activate in order to actually smile. There's a saying about how it takes more muscles to frown, right? So why not smile? **Well, for starters it can be hard for a number of reasons: frustration at work, disturbance in the personal realm, or it just might be a very busy day.**

Let me tell you a story. It starts with my parents, as oh so many of my stories do. Both of them are deaf. Advances in technology (i.e. texting, Skype, online messengers) have really increased the ease in which we are able to communicate. I like to think they are those edgy parents who have always known how to text, use abbreviated lingo, and of course, emojis. For my father, who is one of the most loving, outgoing, and extroverted people I know, one might think digital communication or lack of verbal language would hinder or limit his ability to express his love for others. I believe it has actually done the opposite. My father possesses the ability to make anyone feel welcome, loved, or listened to in a heartbeat. Deaf or hearing. **His smile, his laugh, these are all signatures of who he is.**

This ability to just smile at anyone is a trait I have always admired in my father and something I have tried to emulate in my life. I do this because I know that I never really know what someone else might be experiencing that day.

For the past three years my family has been engaged in a high conflict divorce. My mother has been entrenched in a legal battle to divorce my ex-stepfather. It is taking longer to get through this divorce than it did for me to obtain my master's degree and work a year professionally. This divorce has opened up a lot of secrets we (my mom, brother and myself) kept through their decade-long marriage: secrets of emotional and physical abuse, unhappiness and deceit. If you ask almost anyone who knew me through high school or college, they would have no idea of the severity of what my family was experiencing every day.

On any given day, there are an insane amount of emails exchanged between my grandparents, aunt, mom's best friend, mom and myself about what is going on (this is one time I say thank goodness for reply all). The topics range from anything from a recent custody negotiation to degrading and threatening emails from my ex-stepfather to the next vacation my grandparents are going on. I am pretty used to this now. I am used to seeing the emails, the messages from lawyers and the financial statements. I am used to anticipating a court decision to see it be postponed (we can talk about the failures of the family court system another day), seeing signs of a positive end and being highly disappointed. **Ultimately, it is a roller coaster of emotions, and I do my best to process it all.** I haven't mastered it. I have talked to counselors. I talk to friends, my partner and my family, but at the end of the day, there are days where it is hard to work through. It is something that is still hard to talk about. There are days where this weight feels unbearable and any added stress or unkindness from someone can feel like the final blow. **On the other side of that proverbial coin, on those difficult days when I encounter a smile from someone, even just a sliver of a smile from someone walking between buildings, that moment, that smile can be life-sustaining.**

This is why I try to always smile.

I, just like them, do not know what battles they're fighting. It can be hard to know what load one another is carrying every day. We owe each other kindness. The world we live in can be harsh, jobs stressful, and our coworkers and students may be dealing with things that are weighing them down. When we decide to roll our eyes or treat others with disrespect we might be adding fuel to the fire, adding weight to an already heavy load. Our world can also be bright, our vocations rewarding, and we can offer a kind smile. College and university campuses should be places of care and places of smiles. Mother Teresa said, "Every time you smile at someone, it is an action of love, a gift to that person, a beautiful thing," and I believe it is true. It can be hard some days to smile – I get that – but those days when it costs you nothing, it could mean the world to someone else.

Smile. Just smile.

Ryan is a first year Residential Learning Coordinator @ValpoResLife. He found a sense of home in his undergrad through his involvement with Res Life during a difficult time in his family life and continues to be inspired to smile because of the work he does. Ryan believes there could never be enough coffee or wine to drink, books to read, or words to say. Connect with Ryan on Twitter @ByeByeRyan

making the call.

Adriane's Story

Making the Call - Adriane Reilly

Hi, my name is Adriane, and I just completed my first therapy session last week. My journey to the big comfy couch with my therapist probably started the day I was born, but I've been calling out for help without knowing it since about October. As I settle into year two after grad school, I'm coming to terms with life as a young adult and newlywed and not doing so well. I've been battling stress, TMJ, tension headaches, control issues, generalized anxiety disorder, unhealthy comparison, self-doubt and perfectionism. Being a talkative person, I vent in the moment here and there to numerous trusted people in my life. Maybe if I got them all in one room to compare stories, they would realize I had been hinting that something was wrong all along. However, I never directly stated how I was feeling and what was bothering me. **In my mind, it was completely out of the question to ask for help.** I convinced myself that everyone was just as busy as I was and that I needed to suck it up and manage things on my own. So I withdrew from family and friends and got to controlling things.

You see, I tend to compartmentalize and sub-divide areas of my life. I have categories for everything: work (sub: registered student orgs, new student orgs, supervision, policy, social media, departmental programs, committees), relationships (sub: my partner, family, old friends, new friends), home (sub: laundry, cooking, dishes, tidy rooms, bills) and so on. I can manage without anxiety if the majority of the compartments are under (my) control. **But once things shift and I start to get the feeling that multiple compartments and/or subcompartments are headed toward chaos, anxiety takes hold.** I am easily irritated, my breathing quickens, and my heart flutters. I feel a tightness in my chest, my brain feels full, and I want to run away and hide in bed.

I would tell myself, "But you can't hide in bed. You're a working student affairs professional. It would be shameful to admit you can't handle stress. Student affairs professionals value handling stress so much that it's an interview question. Suck it up and show 'em you can do this."

From October through March things piled up until I finally broke down. From the back corner of my brain, a few voices whispered. Ed Cabellon's 2014 Student Affairs Health Pledge encouraged me to talk "with loved ones about how I am feeling." Amma Marfo's story about managing her anxiety demonstrated that successful student affairs professionals also live with the feelings I'm experiencing. Stacy Oliver-Sikorski's pleas for the #sachat community to shine more light on mental health issues affirmed there's no shame in seeking help. Closer to home, I heard the voices of coworkers who also sought therapy during stressful times.

So I made the call and attended my first appointment. **I feel amazing.** Life didn't magically improve overnight, but I am actively correcting how I react to my anxiety. Upon my therapist's suggestion, I have been keeping a worry journal to clear my mind. I write whenever I need to in whatever format feels natural including stream of consciousness, bullet points, to-do lists and questions. I'm learning to regularly examine my mind and heart to ask, "How am I feeling?" and, "What am I needing?" I'm counting the days until our next appointment and look forward to what our future conversations will uncover. **I feel at ease knowing that I will have a non-judgmental resource to help me understand my mind and improve my relationship with myself and others.**

And now, when people who may have seen me at my most vulnerable ask me how I'm doing, I reply, "Yeah, I'm okay. I'm going for therapy now." **I refuse to hide behind stigma in hope that my decision to openly seek help inspires someone else to find their own path to mental wellness.**

On May 13, we clicked "publish," and the story of my mental health concerns went public for all to read. Despite Sue's reassurance that I had her support and that of the other "Committed" authors, I was nervous about how sharing my story would impact my life. From the day I agreed to participate in the initiative, my mind raced with concerns.

> *What would they think of me? Would I be perceived as weak? Would publishing my story cost me a job in the future? Would people act differently around me now?*

Bigger than my fear, however, was the motivation to connect with that one other young professional stuck deep in the same self-destructive spiral I had been in only weeks before. When I was feeling desperate and alone in my struggle, I grew acutely aware of our society's tendencies to put up facades and act like everything is okay. As my anxiety simmered under the surface (undiagnosed), I yearned to know that someone out there was feeling like me.

Over the last few months, my opinion grew stronger. Putting up a facade is a disservice to everyone. I resolved to live a mission to be my most authentic self to model the way for others. I knew that telling my story was important whether it helped one person or one thousand.

> *It didn't matter what anyone thought of me. I am not my mental disorder. I may have some weak moments, but the love in my heart and the value of my work speak louder than moments of vulnerability. If this*

ever cost me a job, not only would it be illegal on the hiring party's part, but would I really want to work in an environment that didn't support my mental health needs? Nope. Perhaps I needed people to act a little differently around me- to remind me to be gentle with myself or to correct their false assumptions of me.

So I breathed through the flutters of my heart at 4 PM on May 13 as I stepped out from the shadows of stigma and into the light. The response was remarkable.

Fellow student affairs professionals- colleagues and strangers alike- thanked me via Twitter, DMs, or comments on my post, saying they saw much of their own story in mine. As others encouraged me for finally reaching out for help, my little whisper of a story grew louder.

What surprised me most was the response of those closest to me. I shared a link to my story with my non-student affairs best friends, thanking them for their support along the way. One friend said it was very helpful in understanding my mind. I felt comforted as she offered her support and prayers for me. Other best friends reminded me that they loved me and reassured me it's okay to ask for help.

Current and former co-workers said they were proud of me. They thanked me for speaking out because they felt like they were the only one. Most notably, one of my role models at my institution (who I didn't think my story would reach) contacted me to commend my courage for sharing my powerful story. She said she understood the feeling of anxiety and perfectionism all too well. I never expected her to say that! To me, she was perfect and had it all together. I suppose it was my authenticity that opened the door for hers. I'm glad to know that side of her now.

Overall, my #SAcommits experience has been validating. If I didn't get the chance to say it in the moment, thank you for your retweets, shares, likes, comments, e-mails, texts, warm wishes, prayers, etc. Your support has been palpable and I'm grateful for you. I look forward to sharing the story of my treatment on this blog as I do my part to stomp out the stigma of mental illness.

I'll leave you with encouragement to be authentic and vulnerable with one another, because you never know who needs that part of you.

 Adriane Reilly uses nail art as stress relief. She works with student organizations and sings in a post-collegiate a cappella group. She's an ESFJ. Adriane loves cooking, singing, reading, skylines, talking with her hands, & purple. Say hello and start a convo with Adriane at @adrianereilly and visit her Tumblr as she shares mental health information that inspires her along with other personal tidbits and reflections at http://adrianereilly.tumblr.com.

mental health
in the
STATE OF THE WORKING POOR.
Jessica's Story

Mental Health in the State of the Working Poor - Jessica Fantini

Though my story isn't pretty, I am more than willing to
share it now. I believe with any story you have to start at the
beginning; here is a short version of my background so the
rest of the story makes a little more sense. I'm the youngest
of two in a single parent household. My parents were never
married and separated before I was born. I grew up on
welfare, and we had Salvation Army Christmases. We were
poor. Every time I asked my mother to buy me something,
she told me to be patient and wait because maybe we'd be
able to get it next time when it was on sale. We struggled as a
family to be financially stable for most of my childhood. I
thought that a college education was the right choice and
that it came with financial stability. I dreamed of the old
"rags to riches" story. I was wrong. I know my mother loves
me, but she was completely useless when it came to
understanding anything about college and the financial
responsibility of it. I took out loans upon loans just to afford
to go to the school that I picked, and unfortunately I had no
guidance on what that would mean in the long run.

What does this have to do with mental health? More than you would think. **As an adolescent I had difficulty with depression and anxiety.** I never said anything to anyone and wasn't diagnosed until I told myself enough was enough. **I was 27 by the time I was able to discuss my issues with my doctor.** I had been dealing with my mental health for fifteen years before seeking help. I had gone through different periods of time when things were okay, not okay, and devastating. I also drank to avoid dealing with issues then. Since alcohol is a big thing within student affairs, it was easy to do. Things at work just got worse. I never wanted to get out of bed and go to work. I was sick a lot. It was hard to find energy to make a change so I could get better.

I've never wanted to be labeled as weak or as someone with issues. I have issues. I get it. My depression has come and gone over the past year, but because I moved, I haven't brought it up with my new doctor yet. **I want to, but I want to actually find a therapist. I'm just afraid of how much money it will cost me.**

Before I moved, it was a $25 copay per visit. I couldn't afford it then so I never went. I still can't afford it. **Instead of**

46

thinking the issue with mental health is being brave to own it and speak up about it, I think the issue is sometimes about those who truly can't afford it. I've found my strength in sharing my story and struggle with mental health. I just need to figure out how to afford the help.

How do we help those who need help? I knew going into student affairs would not make me rich. I didn't enter the field for the money. **I've always wanted to help people, but helping others doesn't always allow me to help myself.** Although I graduated college - twice - and have a steady job, I'm part of the working poor. I didn't talk about my mental health because I was afraid. I surely don't talk about my financial situation, as that, too, is an area of embarrassment for me. I shouldn't have to feel shame for living paycheck to paycheck, but I've found that some people in student affairs can't fathom why that would be the case. I've had people insist that it's my budgeting skills that are the issue and that it can't be the salary and benefits of my position. I don't blame anyone for the decisions I made that got me here, but I also don't think that it has everything to do with those decisions either. We are the people who are consistently supporting students, giving them resources and allowing them to find their voice, but what about our colleagues who have similar struggles?

Why do we ignore them? **Why do we think it can't happen to us?** Something that has stuck with me since grad school was a story from one of my professors who witnessed a shooting of a student - you can learn theory in a classroom, but nothing prepares you for a real life tragedy. We have people on the front lines, and yet some of us have health benefits that don't cover therapy. Those same people are in positions like mine that may not offer a salary that enables them to cover co-pays for therapy services. **We need to do better at offering services as well as educating staff on those services as much as we do for students.** I love what I do, but it's hard. How do we make it easier? How do we offer support and understanding to those who need it? Whose responsibility is it?

Jessica Fantini is a Residence Life professional in and has held various entry-level live-in positions over the past six years. She has a BA in Social Work and Counseling and a MS in Education with a specialization in Leadership in Higher Education. Through it all; she has been battling with depression and anxiety. Connect with her at @J_Fantini on Twitter or read her blog at http://jesstini13.blogspot.com/.

How Are You, REALLY?
Shane's Story

How Are You, Really? - Shane Cadden

I believe prioritizing and practicing an authentic ethic of care with students and staff makes me professionally successful because it makes me credible. I've always been the advocate for being your true self and the person who has appropriate but authentic dialogue around the question, "How are you, really?" I never thought that enhancing this authentic dialogue could have resulted from a crisis that happened to me. **That is what happened one particular summer during the housing and residence life training craze when I nearly died from a pulmonary embolism, a blood clot in my lung.**

There was no rhyme or reason to this blood clot; it just happened. I could have died on a random Saturday evening, and I had absolutely zero control. In the weeks and months ahead, the response of my brain and body showed their displeasure with heightened anxiety and panic attacks. **I developed a mental health scare in the form of an anxiety disorder I had never seen the likes of before.**

In the year or two following this incident, many professional and paraprofessional staff consistently asked about my own healing process. I could have never included the part about the anxiety and panic attacks that developed from having no control over nearly dying in my thirties. However, it would not have been authentic to me and to all the other individuals who were practicing their own ethic of care had I not told the real experience. **The mortality and mental health bell rang true for some of them as well, and we had ourselves many teachable moments.**

Never known for ducking the hard questions, I took them on as they came. I answered each person as honestly as I knew how because, whether it came from the gossip to know what happened or the heartfelt fear for many that I almost died, either way it was an opportunity to be genuine while talking about the significance of physical and mental health. I am hardly a fan of the well-known **TMI,** but I do believe greatly in my own version, Talking Meaningfully and Intentionally. In this case, it was about making your physical and mental health needs the priority they should be, no matter one's age. One day I was a happy, healthy, and hopeful 30-something, and then within minutes each of those states were altered.

I am confident that the staff I worked with already knew I valued them and every part of their well-being, including their mental health. This life event thankfully added to the credibility. Not only was "How are you, really?" being asked in what seemed like a more intentional manner by others, **I found so many more staff who grew increasingly authentic when I continued to ask it of them.** Their willingness to be open and receptive about their own physical and mental health needs in how they were was significant. **I'm glad to say that from one horrible and scary time in my life I still found a way to care, while**

at the same time learning to better receive care from others.

I would be remiss if I did not say that there are way too many people to recognize who cared for me during this time period, but you are not only not forgotten, you know I'm always still here to ask "How are you, really?"

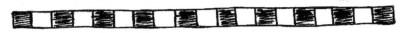

Shane Cadden is an advocate for authenticity & meaning-making, originally from Boston, MA, but currently living in Winter Springs, FL. He received a Bachelor of Arts in English from Stetson University and a Master of Theological Studies/Pastoral Care and Counseling from Vanderbilt University Divinity School. Shane has over 15 years of experience in student affairs and is actively pursuing his next professional role. You can follow or connect with shane @scaddenFNL or at his blog at ridingtheelevator.wordpress.com

WHAT anxiety FEELS LIKE.

Amma's Story

What Anxiety Feels Like - Amma Marfo

Today was the first day this week I felt at ease in the office. Before this morning, the pace of the coming month was revealing itself, and meetings stacked on top of meetings caught up with me. **And in keeping with my goal of expressing vulnerability, I can admit that I had an anxiety attack on Tuesday afternoon.** I know how to ride them out now and what I have to do to make sure I come out of it okay, but it happened.

Another challenge for me is mindfulness, so I try in those moments to remember that it's not going to kill me and concentrate on what I can do to help it pass. I have been asked what my anxious moments feel like; the passage below is my attempt to "write my way out of it" while maybe explaining what frequent yoga, "me time" breaks and a modified diet and supplement regimen are helping me to avoid.

It is an unstoppable and unmistakable quickening of the pulse and breath, coming on suddenly but staying far longer than you would ever expect or hope for;

It is an inability to breathe deeply, with the heaviness of something indeterminate or unknown bearing down on your chest;

It is the tingling of the fingers and the tightening of the shoulders, reaching for something you want to find in your bag or in a drawer; what you're looking for, you can't quite say;

It is the shifting of the eyes, slowly at first, then more and more quickly in search of something to jog the memory of what you might be looking for or needing;

It is the racing of the mind, ruminating and repeating standard tasks in hopes of remembering what you are positive is being overlooked, or what you will say to the person you're sure you're letting down or forgetting;

*It is the desire to close all the doors and pull down the shades, to sit or lie down eyes squeezed shut until the racing stops and the world **slows down**;*

53

It is the gradual understanding that these feelings are both transitory and constant, fleeting and ever present.

It is the acceptance of the fact that no matter how these moments are managed or mitigated, that they may never truly leave. It is the belief that these moments will not define you and do not have to render you powerless between their occasional appearances. It is the faith in the fact that you are bigger than these moments, that they will pass, and that you will be standing when the pulse slows, the breath returns, and the panic subsides.

Amma Marfo is the Assistant Director of Student Activities at Emmanuel College in Boston, MA. She is also a stand-up comedy fan, avid writer, and professional introvert- those last two pursuits culminated in the publication of her first book, THE I'S HAVE IT, in January 2014. Connect with her on Twitter, @ammamarfo or on her blog at ammamarfo.com.

I Carry That Guilt with Me Daily - Deb Schmidt-Rogers

Have you ever had a conversation with a parent that left you shaking your head? I have had plenty, and for a long time the ones that really got me were the ones where parents would tell me, "I think they really need to stay at (insert your college name here) to be successful." I, as the college administrator, had phoned them in the hopes that they would drop everything and get to campus as quickly as they could, because their student was disintegrating in front of my eyes. I don't make these calls whimsically.

But. They. Didn't. But. They. Wouldn't. I now know it was because they couldn't.

I am the parent of a brilliant, creative, super-funny, highly verbal and very sensitive, 17 year old daughter with the most beautiful eyes I have ever seen. She is also bi-polar. She is a joy to be around when she is stable and on her medications. I suspect she was diagnosed about 4 years too late, and I carry that guilt with me daily. I suspect she should have been on medication years earlier, and I carry that guilt with me daily. I have so much guilt about her diagnosis on any given day, that it can paralyze me or reduce me to tears (I am pretty close to those tears as I write).

She had her first hospitalization in her first year of high school. Almost one week inpatient, released with a diagnosis of major depressive disorder and placed on medication. She was bullied after that hospitalization (though we did not know it for many months – and I carry that guilt with me daily), and in her sophomore year, things came to a head. We pulled her out of high school in March and began to homeschool her. Her diagnosis was changed to bipolar and nearly five medications later, she seemed to stabilize. Homeschooling increased her academic confidence. We had a really wonderful summer between junior and senior year. She worked full time, traveled to and from work successfully, saw her therapist weekly, took her meds. She was feeling good...and you know what happens when bipolar people feel good? They think they do not need to be on their medication. We discovered weeks later that she was not taking her meds but was throwing them away.

So what does living with a person with bipolar disorder feel like? Like you are walking on eggshells all the time. Like you are afraid to be in your own home. Like you must weigh each and every sentence that comes out of your mouth because you don't know if that will be the sentence that sets her off. Like you want to live somewhere else. And yes, I carry that guilt with me daily.

My daughter could be having a conversation with me about something innocuous, and I would say the thing that triggered her. She did not like to hear no. She broke things, she threw things, she tore things, she said vile, evil, frightening things. She would tell me afterward that she could feel herself losing control and would tell herself to stop, and the next thing she knew she was throwing the laptop across the room or down the stairs or out the window. The police have been called to my house because her behavior has been so frightening. I have been told that she is going to kill me (and the way that she would do it in great detail), I have been told to never speak to her again. I have been told I am the worst mother ever, I have been told that she hates me more than any person could hate another person. I have been told that I will never, ever see my grandchild. I have heard all of those things hundreds of times, and in between those times, I get punctuated obscenities of the worst kind – words I would never, ever say.

Do you think I am kidding? Have you ever lived with someone who has bipolar disorder?

She disintegrated quickly this past fall when she went off of her medication. She became so out of control, that on October 15th, the police needed to be called. She ran down the street holding a knife and we did not know where she was for four days. She stopped attending school, she stopped communicating. And here is my big confession. My daughter has not lived with us since October 15th. Very few people in my professional circle know this. My own co-workers do not know this. I feel like the worst mother in the world – my 17-year-old daughter does not live with us because she refuses to be med compliant, and we cannot live like we have been for the last two years because we need to be healthy, too. As parents, we are told over and over about unconditional love. I am here to tell you that the line between tough love and unconditional love is razor thin.

I am an advocate for coming out from behind the curtain, and yet, here I have been – safely behind the curtain for almost seven months. I am afraid of being judged. I don't believe the tweets of support – would you really hire me if you knew I had to deal with this on a daily basis? Do you think it would distract me from my work?

My daughter and I are working toward a relationship. We speak, we call, we text. We see one another fairly regularly and frequently. I say less, and I am less confrontational than I want to be. She will be a mother in September, and I want, no I need, to be in her life. She is, after all, brilliant, creative, super-funny, highly verbal and very sensitive - my 17-year-old daughter with the most beautiful eyes I have ever seen.

 Deb Schmidt-Rogers is the Director of Residential Education. She is a proud wife and mother and loves to sing. You can connect with her on Twitter @dschmidtrogers

NUTELLA and NOT'S
Joe's Story

Nutellas and NOT's - Joe Ginese

"Hey, you look tired. You feeling okay?"
"How are you today?"

Raise your hand if you have ever had someone ask you one of those three questions.

Now raise your hand if your first instinct when asked those questions is to default to how you are physically feeling.

"Thanks, legs are sore but it was worth it."
"Yeah, I'm fine. Just a late night."
"I'm good, and you?"

I'd like to share some thoughts with you about **how we define our fitness and our wellness.** The two go hand in hand in most cases, but while one is embraced and cheered for the other is given a slight head nod and a subtle pat on the back.

JOE'S TWO MODES

As someone who usually operates at extremes, when I am on I am on. I am hitting my flow to the point of a euphoric blackout where I'm not realizing what I am doing or saying. Very little thinking takes place. It is like an out of body experience that feels like nothing else. A perfect example of that is my Pecha Kucha from ACPA. I got off the stage physically shaking with adrenaline and asking myself, "What the heck just happened?!" I hit my flow.

The other end of that extreme is when I am down I am down. No idea sticks. Curiosity quivers in a corner of my mind. My shoulders feel as though they are magnetic and are trying to connect to my toes. Globs of Nutella seem like a good idea no matter the time of day. (Arguably, that isn't necessarily a sign of being down since globs of Nutella are always a good idea.) **Imposter syndrome becomes an ailment that handicaps the slightest bit of motivation or daydreaming.**

I point this out because I see a difference in how we support one another with our physical health and how we support one another with our mental health. **Both are in the category of wellness yet physical health gets the red carpet while mental health has to sneak in the side door.** Physical health within student affairs has Facebook pages, Facebook groups, and a hashtag (#SAfit) while mental health has...an occasional appearance as a topic on a chat poll. This is changing because I think the momentum and attention that #SAcommits has harnessed will serve as the bedrock of these conversations to continue on larger and smaller scales.

The conundrum here is that people don't know how to talk about wellness in a holistic manner. Student affairs can often be bashed for being martyrs when talking about the hard parts of our responsibilities and duties. We are celebrated when something goes extremely well but not celebrated when something extremely difficult was handled properly. I'm not saying that in place of 13.1, Spartan Race, 5K stickers on your car you should have stickers announcing "I survived a 40 hour shift of residence life duty that included a student death." **What I am saying is that we need to be better at supporting each other, and we need to be empowered and confident enough to build our pyramids of support.** You cannot do that without being honest with yourself and with your confidants.

I'm lucky to have friends who on a daily or weekly basis will send a message saying, "How are you doing?" and know they mean it in a deeper way. They aren't asking it as someone behind the counter asks it as part of a social ritual; they are asking it because they want the truthful answer. Part of that is the luck of meeting great people and the other part of that putting in the effort to build that mutual trust and relationship that fosters that type of care and concern. Those parts are only possible, for me, because I married a partner who taught me how to do both.

Mental wellness workouts mean practicing reflection, gratitude, and peace. These can be done by journaling, letter writing, and shutting off your phone. **Mental wellness isn't just a matter of what you can do, it is also a matter of what you choose NOT to do.** You can choose NOT to say yes to that next committee opportunity. You can choose NOT to volunteer to help with an event. You can choose NOT to attend a networking event or social as long as in place of those things you are choosing to do something that refreshes, revitalizes, and/or relaxes you. Our brains are one of our most important muscles, if we work it too hard it can sprain or get pulled. A friend and I like to call this out by declaring, "I have the dumb." It basically means that you are mentally spent and your brain has stopped functioning on a higher level.

Yes, life is short. Yes, you could/should carpe all the diems, most of the time. Just realize that you have to stop to refresh and renew just like a NASCAR racer has to pit stop for fuel, tires, and adjustments. It is all part of the process and the journey. I mention in my Pecha Kucha that we need to dig deeper with our questions and our networking. Digging deeper means taking conversation beyond the surface, which means not being afraid to ask how someone is mentally handling a situation or celebration and in return, not being afraid to speak up. It also takes time, which means standing still and turning down other things while you sit and dig in.

So grab your Nutella and make some time for someone in your life that may need to hear the question, "How are you really doing?" and be prepared to dig in.

 As an MBA trained, entrepreneurial minded, and education focused professional, Joe has taken his curiosity to task in efforts to advocate for the reinvention of learning experiences and innovation within higher education. Some call Joe an instigator while others describe him as an innovator. He considers himself a champion for change. He tweets most with @JoeGinese, writes sometimes at www.joeginese.com, and is most likely to be tweeting, writing or reading about psychology, sociology, consumer behavior, creativity, learning, teaching, and storytelling.

64

the simple life
Jessa's Story

The Simple Life - Jessa Carpenter

Somewhere along the way, life gets complicated. When I look back at my early teens and the amount of anxiety I felt about my hair, boys, social events, grades, boys, my weight, and OMG BOYS, I laugh at how easy I unknowingly had it. Even in the years since then I have been incredibly lucky.

Last spring was the first time that I had to face my complications head on, and that was HARD. **I was in my last semester of my student affairs graduate program and right smack dab in the middle of my job search when my little sister got really sick and quickly died.** When I say smack dab, I mean it. I had to cancel a second interview at ACPA because of a phone call just one hour before it telling me that my sister was in a coma. I had to cancel my volunteer shifts at NASPA because literally the day after my TPE interviews were over, she passed. All of the anxiety and stress that is associated with a nationwide job search, comprehensive exams, graduating, moving away from family and friends, and either selling or renting out our house immediately doubled with her illness, then tripled with her death. Here is what my brain looked like:

ImissJamie.WILLANYONEHIREME?!?omg what if someone hires me? Where will we live, when will we have to move, should we rent or sell, when would we have to list our house, what if it sells before we are ready to move, what do we do then?Ineedmymommy. My mom, is she ok?! She just lost her daughter. I'm an only child. OMGimanonlychild. I need to go to class. What is due? I forgot about that. WHAT IF I DON'T GRADUATE? I'm so hungry, I hope someone feeds me soon. icantfeedmyself. WILL ANYONE HIRE ME? why are people staring at me? thisissoweird thisissoweird thisissoweird ImissJamie.

The stress was too much. **It was difficult for me to make even the most simple decisions for myself, like what to eat or what to wear.** Writing final research papers was close to impossible. I had a third interview for a job I really wanted the day after my sister's services, sick as a dog, because I just couldn't figure out if I would disqualify myself by trying to postpone (Pro tip: I should have postponed). Everyone around me had these sad eyes when they looked at me that made me want to either punch them or cry. One of the strangest things was that I brought Jamie up all of the time, in the most awkward of ways. "You like red? My dead sister had this red hat that she wore everywhere. It was hilarious." I still do that sometimes, but I am more used to the weird looks I get for it.

With all of these emotions piling up around me, there was only one option: to simplify things, all the things. I began to find a lot of hidden messages in my interactions with friends and in my favorite financial independence blog and I listened. Losing a 24-year-old sibling is the most awful thing. I never could have prepared for it, even if it was not so sudden. But I also could not have possibly imagined that this horrible thing would end up making my life a little better. **Her death gave me the space and the permission to readjust my priorities, which has directly impacted my quality of life.**

Now I focus on spending time with the people who enrich my life. My partner and I thought carefully about the life that we want to lead, and we are taking immediate steps to make that happen. **We are getting rid of things and spending more time together.** It's a journey that I am still on, but as a result my life feels slower, more genuine, and my emotions (while not always positive) are less complicated. Feels are so much easier when the background noise is dimmed.

 Life is short, way too short. My priorities may look different than a lot of people's, but try to stop yourself if you start to judge when someone else's priorities are different than yours. You never know what got them there.

Jessa is the student services coordinator for a brand new online dual enrollment program. She loves awkwardly mentioning Jamie and her red hat, growing food in her backyard and time well spent with loved ones. Connect with her on Twitter @jessacarpenter or read more about her experiences (and see some rad pictures)on her blog.

Finding my Silence through Sound - Annie Greaney

Even before I was diagnosed with post-traumatic stress disorder (PTSD), depression and anxiety, I found peace in music. Through this organized and sometimes unexplainable noise I am able to find silence. **Even though I have started therapy, nothing has yet to compare to listening and expressing myself through music, especially when I find myself becoming ungrounded.**

When I was growing up I didn't have a good relationship with my family and started using music then as a way to escape any fighting in my house or the pressure placed on me to perform well in sports. Hitting in the batting cages was so much more therapeutic if I played some Dave Matthews. When my parents fought and I could pop in my headphones and listen to classical to drown it out I felt like I was safer, transported to another place. I used music throughout college and graduate school to write papers and flesh out ideas for my work in student affairs. Every day in my office I had and continue to have 8-tracks or Pandora playing. I have always used it as a way to ground myself.

   **I find it easier to find a connection with music and
let go in a safe space than it is for me to pinpoint the
root of my anxiety or PTSD when I feel like I'm
losing control.** If I get into a fight with someone or
something happens that throws me completely off, the best
thing I can do is pop in my headphones and go for a walk.
Part of calming myself down is the physical activity, **but
mostly the music is what helps bring me back into
myself.** I can find a song or playlist that really speaks to
how I feel or how I want to feel and connect with it, which
helps me push past the anger to allow me to process my
thoughts and feelings more fully. The people that are closest
to me know how important music is to me; when my iPod
broke, I was immediately presented with two more. I thought
my world was unraveling when I had no way to carry music
with me. **Having people that understand my need for
music means they understand the most important
part of me.** Music is also a way that I am able to express
how I am feeling to others. I haven't always been the best at
communicating how I feel or what I think. Words are not my
strong suit, so being able to use music to express myself has
not only been therapeutic, it has also helped others to better
understand how I feel and how to help me. When I have

something important to say to someone in my personal life, I am always able to find a song or playlist that speaks exactly to how I am feeling or what I want to say. I don't know of any other medium that is able to do that. When **I play someone a song, I feel as though it is really me talking to them in a voice I can't find for myself.**

 My struggle with mental illness is present every day in my life, and so music is always present, as well. Without it, I don't know how far I would have made it. Perhaps not a career in student affairs, perhaps not graduate school, perhaps not even college. **The one thing about music is that I have control, but I also know it will always be there for me.** I can choose what to listen to and when. I can choose to be grounded. I can choose to relive memories from the past connected to songs, or I can find something new that connects with me in a different way that I have never experienced before. Whatever I need, music can provide that sense of connection for me, whether it be with myself or conveying feeling to someone else. **We live and survive by how we connect to others, and my connection happens more intensely, more accurately, and more purposefully, through music.**

 I'm Annie Greaney (pronounced Gray-nee). I was born and raised in Massachusetts where much of my family still resides (the rest live in Ireland). I am a 3rd generation Irish-American. I received my BS in Youth Development from Springfield College and received my MA in Student Affairs in Higher Education from Indiana University of Pennsylvania. I am currently a new student affairs professional living the dream as a Residence Director in California. I am most interested in first generation programs, mental health in higher education, and student transitions and retention. I was first diagnosed with a mental illness in November 2013. You can connect with me on twitter @AnnieGreaney

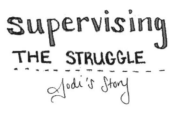

Supervising THE STRUGGLE

Jodi's Story

Supervising the Struggle - Jodi Langsfeld

As a student affairs professional, I believe it is pivotal we create an environment that is safe and supportive for our student body. I believe we are the people they should think of turning to when they need something...almost anything. And, even when we can't personally provide them what they need, we are still here to help. We educate them on what resources are available to them, who to call, where to go; we can even make these connections for and with them. **This is our job and an expectation I have for any member of the team with whom I work.**

The question I pose is **what do we do when a member of our own team, the team that is creating this environment for our students, is struggling and not**

asking for help? What role do we play? The members of a student affairs team know the resources, they know the "players", they know what they need to do. Don't they?

I'd like to think it was that simple, but maybe it isn't. The reasons are many. Perhaps that individual has never sought help before. They may feel they should be able to manage on their own because they always have. Maybe they are concerned about their job, wondering if the perception will be that they can't handle their personal life, so how can their colleagues trust they will handle the needs of a student body? Maybe their family validates their job because they are offering help to others but don't personally support using resources like that. Maybe they assume the available resources are for the students but not the employees. Maybe it is a financial concern, and they can't imagine having another bill to pay. Perhaps it is that they are emotionally drained after dealing with students all day and just can't find the energy to deal with anything else. No matter if it is one of the many valid concerns above, or one not listed, **the real question is what can we do?**

I think most people want to help others when they see someone who needs it. As a peer, you can check in with them, see if they want to talk, encourage them to reach out to someone, access a support structure they already have established or create a new one, even simply let them know you are there for them. **As a team supervisor, the relationship is slightly different.** You want to do everything you would for a student or a peer, but you also need to balance the needs and demands of the department and the student body with that team member.

How do you balance legal concerns, an individual's workload and the running of a department with an individual's mental health and the demands life places on all of us? **I think it is important to understand that every**

situation and every individual is different, but at the core, I believe everyone is looking for the same thing: support and understanding. The next question is how do you successfully achieve providing that? I have developed three questions I consistently ask a member of my team when I am worried about them:

Question 1) "Are you OK? No, are you really OK?" People will answer this question very quickly, and most of the time that is fine. But when you are worried about someone, you need to take a deep breath, and you need to have them take a deep breath so they understand you are sincerely asking the question, not simply doing what is socially expected.
Question 2) "Is there anything I can do?" This has to be asked sincerely, and you have to be prepared for the answer. They may ask for nothing, or they could ask for emotional support and your understanding while they are struggling, or even time off.
Question 3) "Do you understand that I am here to support you however I can? I will do anything in my power to help you, but I can only do something if you identify how I can help you."

The responses to these questions can be endless, and until an individual is ready to accept help, there is nothing we can do but continue to try to support them, continue to ask them questions and continue to remind them that we are here, and they are valuable. **Sometimes all they need to know is simply that. Sometimes they need a lot more.** As a team leader, it is my responsibility to ask questions, to ensure that my team knows that they should feel the same way the students feel about student affairs: it is a safe environment where they can come to feel supported. I hope every member of my team sees that what they have been striving to provide the student body is the same thing they have around them: good people who sincerely want to help them.

Jodi Langsfeld works as the Associate Dean for Student Affairs at the Hofstra North Shore-LIJ School of Medicine. Her previous experience includes serving as the Director of Graduate Medical Education She has been actively involved in residency and fellowship education at a national level for many years. Jodi believes in an open door policy, always having a full stock of M&Ms and creating safe spaces for her students and staff.

GRAD SCHOOL SELFIE

Monica's Story

Grad School Selfie - Monica Fochtman

I drew this picture of myself in spring 2007 when I was a full-time doctoral student. It was part of an assignment for our qualitative research methods class. I remember being excited to draw this picture because I thought that my fellow graduate students' self-portraits would look similar, and I looked forward to kvetching about grad school life when we shared them in our small groups. At the time, my other roles included mother, wife, part-time graduate assistant, and daughter and sister to a far-away family that was in crisis. These roles were obviously weighing heavily on me and my psyche. **Clearly the person in this photo was not well. I was not well.**

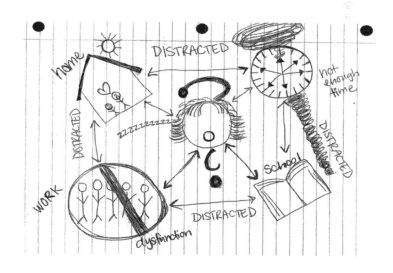

77

What shocked me was that other students in class did not have drawings that looked like mine. Sure, doctoral life is hard, and we were all dealing with the pressures of work, assistantships, families and too much reading. So much reading. But the other drawings looked..."normal." No one else had question marks or the words "distracted" written all over their page. My friends were stressed, but they were not in distress.

Looking at this self-portrait spurred me on to seek help.Thankfully, I had gone to therapy once before so I knew how it benefitted me and subsequently, my other relationships. Having an objective person to talk to was very helpful for me. It was a safe place where I could talk freely without judgment about my perceived failures as a mother and PhD student. **Therapy helped me hit the reset button and gave me tangible coping skills that I needed to manage my runaway thoughts and feelings.**

Therapy worked for me. I would go for a few months, get "better," and then stop going. This was okay at first. **But these feelings of being overwhelmed and paralyzed would always creep back in.** Always.

After my son was diagnosed with cancer, they kicked in full force, and I got myself back in to see someone. Luckily, the person I found had specialized training helping families deal with illness and loss. She let me cry. She let me get really, really angry. And most important, she gave me a name for this darkness that always seemed to find me. I remember sitting in her office one day, and I said, "Why do I keep ending up in this place? I always need to come back here." **She was the first person in my life to tell me that "this darkness" is called anxiety and depression. And it's not my fault.**

When I finally had a name for what I was experiencing, **I felt...relieved.** Sweet, sweet relief. The truth is, I have felt this way for most of my life. Looking back on my late 20s and early 30s, I can now see patterns of behavior. Periods of incredible activity and productivity, followed or preceded by valleys of exhaustion and inactivity. **I thought that this is how everyone felt.** I thought this is what it meant to be east-coast, high-achieving and high-strung. And what was necessary to cope as such.

Since my diagnosis, I have done a lot of research about anxiety and depression. **The biggest lesson I have learned that I hope to share with others is that depression is not logical.** It's chemicals. My brain is wired differently. I need to deal with my chemicals differently. And I need to give myself permission to negotiate life on my terms.

I can shave my head - twice - and raise money for childhood cancer research, but the mere thought of training for another 5K sends me into a tailspin. I tried sleeping in my workout clothes to inspire myself to exercise in the morning, and I ended up having a panic attack. Not logical. It doesn't make sense. It just is. I can stand alone on stage and read from the very bottom of my heart about our family's journey with cancer, but it took me two weeks to write this blog post, and technically, I submitted it a day late. Traffic makes me nervous, but I can drive twelve hours to New Jersey if I know that my niece's first birthday party is waiting on the other side. See? Not logical in any way.

In a way, I am proud of these things. Do I wish that I didn't wrestle with anxiety and depression? Of course. But that is not an option for me. I was depressed. I have depression. I will always deal with it. It is what it is, and I am who I am. **Giving it a name and arming myself with tools to face it head on have made all the difference for me.**

Thanks for listening.

 Monica Marcelis Fochtman grew up in NJ and went to college in Boston- the home of her heart. She earned her PhD from Michigan State University in 2010 and currently works in academic advising. Her consulting & speaking interests are focused on: mid-career women and work-life negotiation, the MBTI, and advocacy for childhood cancer awareness and research funding. She is the mom to six and eight year old boys who are the source of all joy and most of her gray hairs. She negotiates motherhood, being a mid-career professional, and the Midwest at her blog: musingsfromthemiddle.com. She also tweets about all of those things @monicamfochtman.

I'M A PERSON, TOO.

Jason's Story

I'm a Person, Too - Jason Meier

 It was my rallying cry. If a victim needs something, help them. Sort out the forms and receipts and paperwork later. If you're alive and have a roof, you sit in a place of privilege. It's your duty as a human to help those who have lost everything. **Help people first. It became a mantra which would drive my reactions during any times of crisis.**

 On April 15, 2013, I found myself blocks away from the finish line of the Boston Marathon, there to support and cheer on students running the marathon.

 The hours that followed were traumatizing as I attempted to get away from Boylston St. and back to my home. Phone lines were jammed. My phone's battery was dying. I tweeted and Facebooked my status, trying to remain calm. We didn't know what would happen next, and the panic was real. That night, I stayed away from TV, the footage of the attack mixing with images ingrained in my brain.

APRIL 15. 2013

#BOSTONSTRONG

WHAT PTSD CAN LOOK LIKE.

GOTTA TAKE CARE OF THIS GUY TOO. ♥

But I put on a brave face because that's what I was supposed to do. "People come first," I said over and over. I was there for other people. I was there for students, staff and friends impacted by this disaster. I threw myself into volunteer projects and work because people came first.

I blogged about it and was called brave.
I tore up an #sachat about supporting others in a time of crisis and was called a hero.
I was interviewed by dozens of newspapers and TV stations about the #BostonStrong phenomena. But what I never did was think about myself. **I wouldn't admit that I wasn't okay.** And I wasn't okay.

I know what **post-traumatic stress disorder (PTSD) is**, but I never thought I'd be impacted by it. PTSD creeps into you in weird ways:

The first time you walk by the Boston Public Library on Boylston St., and it takes all you have not to vomit on the sidewalk.

Go on a family vacation to a historic fort. A cannon goes off every hour. You freak the hell out every hour on the hour.

The moment you see a friend on the one year anniversary day and you start sobbing as you embrace in a hug.

Many of us in student affairs view ourselves as helpers and healers. We serve others before we serve ourselves. **But in times of crisis, we have to serve ourselves.** We have to help and heal our own hearts and souls before we can be good to others.

In the days following the marathon, I threw myself into work as a way to avoid the situation at hand. It wasn't healthy or sustainable. I needed to take the time to heal myself. I needed to talk to a professional about my struggles.

I know that now. **People will always come first for me, but now I understand I'm a person, too.**

 Jason Meier is the Director of Student Activities at Emerson College, located in the heart of downtown Boston. Jason's heart is still a l ittle banged up after the Boston Marathon Bombings in 2013 but he is and will always be #BostonStrong. Drop him a line on Twitter at @jasonrobert or on his blog at jasonrobert.net.

I Am Going to Live with It - Clare Cady

As I write this, I check in with myself and recognize that I am manic. I've been manic for well over a week now…I probably will be for a few days more. I can feel the start of a new phase in the cycles of my bipolar disorder creeping in. It's the worst part to come – the part where my body feels like it is vibrating with too much energy and not enough all at the same time. It's the withdrawal - the start of the low. **Interestingly enough, the low feels better than the transition.** For now, I push myself to focus in spite of my heightened attention and breathe. Breathing in, I know I am alive. Breathing out, I smile. Thanks, Thich Nhat Hanh.

I was diagnosed with bipolar disorder two-and-a-half years ago; six months after that I started taking medication. I was so afraid to start meds – a holdover from when I was a kid and saw a TV show where one of the main characters was "manic depressive." She was this quiet, dull woman who stopped taking her medication and went off the deep end. Since my mental illness did not send me off the deep end (I am fortunate to this point to have had mild symptoms compared to some), **the thing that made me scared was not the mania, but the way that I was shown meds would impact me.** I did not want to be quiet or mousy or dull. I wanted to remain vibrant and cheerful and funny. **Would taking meds mean the end of who I was?** That's why it took me six months – my therapist had to convince me to try.

 Being on medication does not stop the symptoms, but it does make them calmer and more manageable – and I am aware of them now. When I am gripped by an incredible urge to quit my job, bike to Alaska, hunt a bear to its den, and write a book about it, all without sleeping...I can safely assume that this is fueled by mania. When I have the urge to quit my job, buy a house in the woods, make a nest inside, and stay in there forever with a stockpile of chocolate and bacon...I can safely assume that is fueled by depression.

 I used to not be able to discern that, and the chances of my being consistent were next to nil. Until I was 32, I'd never gone more than a month brushing my teeth, putting on pajamas, and sleeping every night. When I did it for a whole year I was elated. I've lived in the same place for the longest amount of time since I moved out of my parents' house at 18 (almost three years). To give an example of the difference, from 2006-2009 I moved fourteen times. Jobs, relationships, apartments – all of these were things I could not commit to because the emotional, mental and physical experiences of my bipolar roller coaster made me feel that I had to make a change in order to relocate control. **I think about how much money and energy that took, and I wonder what resources or roles I would have today were I able to be more consistent.**

I still struggle. I'm not going to lie. **One of my biggest challenges has been coming to accept that just getting a diagnosis and going on meds does not mean that my problem is solved.** I am going to be bipolar for the rest of my life. I am going to live with it. Sometimes the thought of that is just exhausting. However, I have also been given a tremendous gift of finding pleasure in things I never did. I had no idea that sleep was so amazing!!! I either found it completely useless and a waste of my time to even try, or it was something I did to excess without ever feeling rested. I could not understand why people liked it so much. I have also been able to deepen connections to people and to my work in ways I did not know were possible.

Breaking my silence has helped me, and I am hoping that it will help others, as well.

Clare Cady lives in Corvallis, OR where she serves as Coordinator of the Human Services Resource Center, serving students experiencing poverty, hunger, homelessness, and food insecurity. When not at work, Clare can be found backpacking, cycling, making music, or tasting amazing beverages. Clare is a champion snuggler, and the list of things she would snuggle is long, and i ncludes t-rexes, redwoods, polar bears, manatees, and dogs - ALL THE DOGS.

HITTING THE reset BUTTON.

Renee's Story

Hitting the Reset Button - Renee Dowdy

Last fall I wrote about being at a concert with my husband at The Vic in Chicago seeing the Old 97's (feeling like I'm out of a scene from The Breakup - epic, right?!). I began to panic about having cell phone reception in the theater. Staff in my department expected that I respond to my residential communities 24/7 during the academic year. I kept looking at my work phone, and that's when the panic came over me like a tidal wave. What if I miss a call? Why can't I do this job right? Why can't I seem to do anything right? Why was I hired to do this if I am completely incapable? Were my past six years in residence life just easy - is this the real hard work and I'm failing at it? I'm a failure. An absolute mess. I'm unreliable. I don't have my shit together...and the negative thoughts poured on and on until the music faded in my mind, **and all I saw was the stage in blurry lights as tears fell uncontrollably. I couldn't get it back together.** My husband and I left the concert early. And there I was with more guilt, feeling like I couldn't be at the concert and enjoy an evening out with my husband, but I most certainly did not want to be home. And there it was: trapped, seemingly with no escape, not even within my own mind.

It felt embarrassing to even admit what felt like weakness, let alone how pervasive and damaging my anxiety had become. It was difficult to manage because the constant thought I had was, "What's wrong with me?" While I knew I had people I could talk to, it felt like there was no one I could trust with this burden. After all, aren't everyone's jobs difficult? Isn't everyone busy? Isn't everyone chronically overwhelmed to the point it invades every other facet of life? **Well, the answer is not yes or no but really the impact of anxiety.**

I remember vividly beginning grad school and sitting in orientation sessions with other new grads eager to crack open textbooks and begin classes. One of the faculty shared with us, "In grad school there are three things in your life: your assistantship, your coursework, and everything else. Only two of those will be going well at any given point in time." Her point was taken, and that is where I took up my torch to carry, as I would be damned if my work suffered.

Something we know as student affairs practitioners is Kurt Lewin's infamous equation: that B = f(P, E) or more simply put, **our behavior is the function of us as a person and our environment.** What I discovered is that the issue in the equation, the source of this behavior change, was not me as a person; it was my environment. While it was one that supported ideal behaviors for many, it was one that met my perfect combination of neurotic and over-achieving in a particularly inflammatory way. It was fuel to my anxiety flame.

In my experience with counseling, it was about finding a reset button for myself to identify triggers, recognize coping mechanisms, and also put in place preventative practices that allow me to be my best self. For my situation, I worked with a counselor to find ways to choose behaviors, foods, and physical activity to keep anxious thoughts and behaviors at bay. These improvements have been a journey, but I've found the benefits to far outweigh any opportunity cost. While I had preached to staff for many years that if you're not taking care of yourself, you're not able to take care of others, I had to experience it myself to make some necessary lifestyle changes. **I found my reset button.**

Some aspects of mental health management are within our control, but **work has a major impact of our view of**

who we are, our satisfaction with our lives, and our ability to feel well. For those familiar with Wellbeing, of the five facets Gallup measures, **career has the biggest impact on all of our other areas of wellness.** Meaning, you can be thriving in your community, your relationships, your finances, your physical health, but if your career wellbeing is not in place, the rest will likely pale in comparison. The impact of a stressful work environment where one does not feel engaged or contributing not only leads to an employee feeling disengaged, but it creates a level of mental stress that is worse than prolonged unemployment. Individuals on the front lines and further down the business hierarchy actually feel this impact at a greater intensity than those leading from the top. **We have a responsibility to care for the health and wellness of our employees because our jobs are killing us. Literally.**

Our work environments have the ability to bring out the best of us...and the worst. **One of the most high-impact ways to influence employee wellness and career satisfaction is to be able to give employees a sense of control.** This is an extension of trust and an actionable item that very few of the general "us" in student affairs work to cultivate. When you feel a sense of control in your career, you are provided a sense of calm in your life, and you come to work not afraid of what's happening within your own work environment. What frustrated me about trying to navigate my experiences with anxiety was not the fact that I had the anxiety but the fact that an environment can bring out a part of you that you thought was managed. That an environment can turn things so upside down that it feels as though there is no space to hit reset, to recalibrate, to find another way that works. And as we all know working with colleges and universities, we intentionally design environments on the daily. **Environments matter.** How often do we put intention into creating work environments and consider the impact not only on students but on employees?

Whatever your experience is, we all deserve to work in a space where we can contribute our best work and our best selves. It's good for your health, it's good for those you work around, and frankly, it's good for business. I encourage you to know the triggers that create stress, that send you off-course, that keep you awake at night, that take away your focus, that lead you to a mental health deficit. Find your reset button. Know what resources help you care for yourself in the best way possible and hold to it. Treat it as a personal prescription that you commit to not allowing yourself to neglect and take as instructed. The work will be there tomorrow, and we want you to be there, too.

Renee Piquette Dowdy is the Assistant Director of Education and Curriculum Design for Synergos, AMC, working primarily with the Association of Fraternity & Sorority Advisors (AFA) and the Association of Fraternal Leadership & Values (AFLV). As a Wisconsinite living in the west, she enjoys hot yoga, hiking, leisurely bike rides, and spending time with her Goldendoodle puppy. Renee enjoys writing and speaking on wellness, organizational culture, and professional development strategies. Connect with her on Twitter: @reneepdowdy.

Thick Skin and Therapy - Sue Caulfield

My grandma Millie did her fair amount of worrying as a grandma. I would venture to guess that may be a trait of the Italian women in my family that I very much inherited. One of my fondest memories is of her comforting me when I would cry. "Mi Susan," she would say, holding my hand with her cold, beat up hands. "You need to grow thicker skin. I worry about your heart."

My grandma and I were very close. She was an artist in her own right - making costumes, clothing and the best meals I've ever had. I often think of her and the women in my family when I need a dose of courage. But I never grew that thick skin that my grandma spoke of. **In fact, I turned out quite the opposite.**

My first experience in therapy was in the form of Sister Peggy at St. John the Baptist High School. My second was a campus minister, and my third was another nun. **Each time I attended these sessions, it was due to a precipitating event; something in my life was wrong.** It was clearly defined, I was clearly upset, and I felt justified asking for help. When you have a clearly defined event - my sister's in the hospital, my brother is getting into trouble, my mom was in a car accident, my grandma died, my dad seems like he can't take it - it can be easier to say, "Okay, I need to talk to someone about this before my head explodes."

93

It wasn't until after college that I realized I might actually need to talk about MYSELF in these sessions. In January of 2012, I promised myself that I would give therapy a shot for a minimum of a year. For me, life was at a point where I needed some protected time during the week for myself. I am a feeler with a huge heart and a serious case of the empathys. How I felt was affecting my relationships, my demeanor and, more than I'd like to admit, my job. Maybe I just needed a place to talk, feel, process. A place to just be and not necessarily look for solutions every minute. **Maybe I just needed a professional who I could cry to and admit that I just couldn't hack it sometimes.**

Therapy is a very different experience for everyone. For me, having a trained professional was...well, weird at first. Having someone's eyes staring through you for an entire 45 minutes is unnerving. My first session, I sat there and cried. I don't even think I said anything. Eventually, we got down to business. Michele, my new Friday afternoon standing appointment, was a blessing. She pushed me to ask about everything but made sure it was at my own pace. She never gave me the answers (unless we spoke about a diagnosis or symptoms). She led me on a journey through Dante's Inferno and was quite the Virgil. She let me be angry, upset, guilty, and best of all, happy.

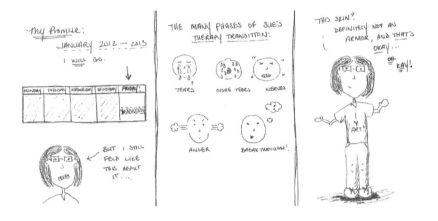

I learned a lot from my Friday afternoon appointments. I learned that there are not always answers, and that's okay. I learned that self-growth is an amazing thing, but it often happens during some...unique? times. I learned that needing therapy doesn't mean you are not strong enough. It doesn't translate to an extra dose of weakness. It doesn't mean you can't get through it on your own. But it's there as a tool if you need it. I learned it's not for everyone...but if it IS for you, then that's okay.

Say it with me now...it's oh. kay.

And if you have the empathys or something a little more formal instead of that thick skin that Grandma Millie talks about? That's okay, too. I promise she will love you just the same.

 Sue Caulfield is an Assistant Director of Student Affairs by day, a small business owner by night and creator of the #Suedle and cofounder of 'Committed.' She thinks in pictures. Her favorite part of her office is her door. In her free time, you can find her with her nose in a book, at a local coffee shop or figuring out how to make this world just a little bit better. Connect with her on Twitter at @_SueCaulfield or in her digital home at suecaulfield.com.

epilogue.

Epilogue - Kristen Abell

Several months after the conclusion of the first Committed e-series in August of 2014, actor and comedian Robin Williams killed himself, bringing mental illness to the forefront again for about a week before something else took its place. This tends to be the cycle with many important topics, but with the Committed series, we hope to keep mental illness in the spotlight and make it an ongoing issue of concern for higher education.

My younger sister once compared depression to slaying dragons. We all have dragons to slay, but most of the time, our dragons are sleeping. For those of us with depression or other mental illnesses, however, our dragons are awake and kicking, and in order to go about the rest of our life, we must first slay them. Sometimes we slay the dragon. Sometimes it slays us. Either way, it takes a hell of a lot of strength and courage to face that dragon every day - whether we win or not.

And for those people that don't get why it's so hard to seek help; for those people who have put up barriers by believing that those of us with mental illness are weak, less than, other; for those people who believe that depression and suicide are merely paths for those who lack courage, well, they have their own dragons, too. Only they're not fighting them - we are.

We treat cancer like a disease, and we treat depression and other mental illness like it's that person's fault for having it. We've sounded the cry before, and we'll sound it again - it is time to take this seriously. It is time to recognize that mental illness is no one's fault and everyone's problem. It is time for us to make this about how society treats mental illness and not about an individual's lack of courage. It is time for people to start slaying their own dragons. Let's make sure we provide them the armor to go to battle.

resources
- - - - - - - - - - -

Resources

Committed Series online resources:
Branch discussing mental health in student affairs
http://branch.com/b/mental-health-in-student-affairs?ref=sidebar#Gdq8pnyuwN8

Storify of #SAcommits chat
https://storify.com/_SueCaulfield/sachat-meets-sacommits-a-chat-on-mental-illness-i

Committed: the Conversation
http://suecaulfield.com/2014/05/19/committed-the-conversation/

Committed: Final thought
http://suecaulfield.com/2014/06/04/committed-a-final-thought/

Additional Resources:
National Suicide Hotline 1-800-273-TALK
http://www.suicidepreventionlifeline.org/

Mental Health.gov
http://www.mentalhealth.gov/

Mental Health Resources
http://www.mhresources.org/

Free Webinars on Workplace Mental Health Promotion:
http://www.mentalhealthcommission.ca/English/issues/workplace/workplace-webinars

List of eating disorders (Free PDF available)
http://www.mind.org.uk/information-support/types-of-mental-health-problems/eating-problems/types-of-eating-disorders/?o=6260#.U_NfrPldX9o

Does health insurance cover mental health treatment?
http://www.nerdwallet.com/blog/health/2014/08/18/health-insurance-cover-mental-health-treatment/

Robin Williams death pushes school to raise awareness
http://www.cbc.ca/news/canada/windsor/robin-williams-death-pushes-schools-to-raise-suicide-awareness-1.2739557

The University of Michigan Public Health Blog – Patterns
http://umsphfrontlines.wordpress.com/2014/08/17/patterns/

The Guardian - Suicide and Silence: Why Depressed Men Are Dying for Somebody to Talk To
http://www.theguardian.com/society/2014/aug/15/suicide-silence-depressed-men

PTSD Jedi - Tsunami Survivor's Journey of Healing
http://www.ptsdjedi.com/

PsychCentral - Postpartum Difficulties Not Just Limited to Depression
http://psychcentral.com/news/2014/08/19/postpartum-difficulties-not-just-limited-to-depression/73783.html

Creating Community Solutions - Text, Talk, Act to Improve Mental Health
http://creatingcommunitysolutions.org/texttalkact

Abell, K. (2012, November 26). The Shame Game. The Student Affairs Collective. Retrieved from http://studentaffairscollective.org/the-shame-game-mental-illness-in-the-profession-of-student-affairs/

Court, S. & Kinman, G. (2008). Tackling Stress in Higher Education. University and College Union. Retrieved from http://www.ucu.org.uk/media/pdf/8/a/ucu_hestress_dec08.pdf

Kinman, G. & Wray, S. (2013, July). Higher Stress: A Survey of Stress and Well-Being Among Staff in Higher Education. University and College Union. Retrieved from http://www.ucu.org.uk/media/pdf/4/5/HE_stress_report_July_2013.pdf

Pryal, K. R. G. (2014, June 2013). Disclosure Blues: Should You Tell your Colleagues About your Mental Illness? Vitae. Retrieved from https://chroniclevitae.com/news/546-disclosure-blues-should-you-tell-colleagues-about-your-mental-illness

Pryal, K. R. G. (2014, July 9). 'She's So Schizophrenic!': How Not to Alienate your Colleagues with Psychiatric Disabilities. Vitae. Retrieved from https://chroniclevitae.com/news/599-she-s-so-schizophrenic-how-not-to-alienate-your-colleagues-with-psychiatric-disabilities

Schneck, K. (2013, November 12). Student Affairs Administrators Get Suicidal, Too. Huffington Post. Retrieved from http://www.huffingtonpost.com/ken-schneck-phd/student-affairs-administrators_b_4236003.html

Shaw, C. & Ward, L. (2014, March 6). Dark Thoughts: Why Mental Health is on the Rise in Academia. The Guardian. Retrieved from http://www.theguardian.com/higher-education-network/2014/mar/06/mental-health-academics-growing-problem-pressure-university

The Student Affairs Collective. (2011, July 22). #SAchat Recap - 7/21/2011 - Mental Health of Student Affairs Professionals. The Student Affairs Collective. Retrieved from http://studentaffairscollective.org/sachat-recap-7212011-mental-health-of-student-affairs-professionals/

The Student Affairs Collective. (2013, October 25). #SAchat Transcript - 10/25/2013 - Mental Well-Being of Student Affairs Pros. The Student Affairs Collective. Retrieved from http://studentaffairscollective.org/sachat-transcript-102513-mental-well-being-of-student-affairs-pros/

Resources addressing faculty mental illness:
Pryal, K. R. G. (2014, August 28). What Do Psychiatrically Disabled Faculty Owe our Students? Vitae. Retrieved from https://chroniclevitae.com/news/680-what-do-psychiatrically-disabled-faculty-owe-our-students

McElroy, L. T. (2013, July 18). Worrying Enormously About Small Things: How I Survive Anxiety and You Can, Too. Slate. Retrieved from http://www.slate.com/articles/health_and_science/medical_examiner/2013/07/living_wi th_anxiety_and_panic_attacks_academia_needs_to_accommodate_mental.html

Saks, E. R. (2012, June). A Tale of Mental Illness - From the Inside. TED. Retrieved from http://www.ted.com/speakers/elyn_saks

Saks, E. R. (2009, November 25). Mental Illness in Academe. The Chronicle of Higher Education. Retrieved from http://chronicle.com/article/Mental-Illness-in-Academe/49233/?cid=vem

Saks, E. R. (2008). *The Center Cannot Hold: My Journey Through Madness*. Hyperion.

Here's To Your
Continued Success!

a Student Affairs Collective book

Made in the USA
Middletown, DE
19 December 2015